when you first called me radha

when you first called me radha
poems

swami sivananda radha

timeless
2005

timeless books
www.timeless.org

© 2005 timeless books

Printed in Canada on acid-free, 30% post-consumer recycled paper.

Library and Archives Canada Cataloguing in Publication

Sivananda Radha, Swami, 1911–1995
    When you first called me Radha : poems / Swami Sivananda Radha.

ISBN 1-932018-07-7
I. Title.
PS8637.I935W48 2005   C811'.6
C2004-906199-2

when you first called me radha
swami sivananda radha

Prayer to Divine Mother   13
(Gebet zur göttlichen Mutter)

My Eyes Are Fixed on Her Beauty   14

The Flute   16

In My Heart Is a Song   19

When Loving You   20

Cremation Ground   21

White Bird   22

Unfinished Poem (circa 1965)   24

Cosmic Intelligence   25

What is Masculine?   26

Enlightenment   27

Light Truth   28

To Find the Entrance   29

Dream Image   30

Yogis, Adepts, Even Gods   32

Three Worlds   33

Excessive Hairsplitting   34

No Ghosts Please   35

Trees Split, Branches Scattered   36

Don't Be Fooled by Emotions   37

All Dissolves Back   38

Consciousness Is Without Sex   39

The Hidden Place   40

Many Old Gods Are Still Around   41

Priests of All Sorts   42

Religion as I Knew It   44

Oh Devotee of Little Intelligence   45

Lovers Have Their Dreams   46

Many Hardships   47

Babies Are Attracted   48

Are You Not Painting Your Own Picture   49

Divine Mother's Many Faces   50

Great Wisdom in Disguise   52

Endless Desert   53

With Greater Awareness   54

I Stood by the Pond   55

Divine Mother, Who Had that Great Blessing   56

The Cosmic Dance   58

Where is My Heart?   59

When You First Called Me Radha   60

Some Souls   62

Afterword   65

About the author   77

PRAYER TO DIVINE MOTHER
Gebet zur göttlichen Mutter

Du, die Du über den Wolken tronst
im blau-silbernen Sternenkleide
neige,
Dein gütiges Antlitz mir zu
gib Ruh'
meinem rastlosen, suchenden Herzen.
Nimm alle Schmerzen
in Deine schützenden, zärtlichen Hände
und lass am Ende
von allem irdischen Tun
meine Seele, göttliche Mutter,
in Deinem Herzen ruhn.

Author's Translation:

Thou, enthroned above the clouds
dressed in night-blue silk, sprinkled
with silver stars,
bend Thy kind face at me
that its sight may give rest
to my restless, searching heart.
Take all pain
in Thy protecting, tender hands
so that on the end
of all worldly work
my soul may find everlasting peace,
Divine Mother, in Thy heart.

MY EYES ARE FIXED ON HER BEAUTY

My eyes are fixed on Her beauty,
my mind wants to dwell
on the flow that comes from Her
filling me with sparks of Her wisdom.
Beauty has no virtue of its own, it just is.
Does the flower know its beauty?
Beauty is in the eye of the beholder.
I long to behold Her beauty forever.
She fills the sky, all stars are the embroidery
of Her robes
even the sliver of the moon holds
Her veil in place.
Her graceful feet are hidden
by the hem of Her dress
and all the silver stars tingle
at every one of Her moves
letting me know She is near.

My ears are open to receive
the sparks of Her wisdom
and my mind is like the air
the flower fills with its fragrance.
All the corners of the earth receive their share.
Beauty invokes magic
and the mind becomes spellbound
for a brief moment
all clatter stops, to be receptive.
Wafts of the indescribable fragrance
of Divine wisdom fills all spaces.
If only the mind could retain that stillness

so the light of the sun can reflect to the moon.
The sphere of light is growing larger and larger
and brighter and brighter
like a thousand suns.
The light streaming forth leaks through
the clouds of the mind
creating a beautiful disk, Divine Mother
in its center.

My eyes are absorbed in Her beauty.
My mind becomes intoxicated
by those streaming rays of brilliant white light.
I command my mind to remember all and everything
to indulge just for a brief moment, just once
with all its power
to recall the smallest detail.
But already the light gets dimmer,
the sun is sinking over the horizon
and my hands are too small to hold the disk
even for a brief moment.
Darkness envelops all surroundings.
Now, I can only wait for Her glorious return.
I am Her child, because She is the Mother of this universe.
She will come again, and some day She might carry me
and take me with Her.

THE FLUTE

The sound of this flute is not of this earth.
It delights and pains my heart
at the same time, tears flow.

When will it end, where will it all go?
Can the trees and the flowers bear the sound of the flute?
Are the dewdrops tears of joy?

The sound of the flute fills my heart,
it must have grown bigger
to contain it all.
Where is my heart and what happened to it?
Krishna has turned it into a pearl
he wears in his nostril – to remember me?

How do I remember him? I don't.
He is always there, not in my heart
but in all cells of my body
that pulse to the rhythm of the flute's melody.

The sound of the flute disturbs my meditation.
My body refuses to stay motionless
my feet want to dance
and the fingers of my hands want to form
lotuses to shower him with.

Hues of light emanate from his body.
Blue has become my favorite colour,
blue sapphires dazzle my eyes.
He is reflected in every facet

all creation is captured in this light
and even a moment becomes eternity.
Have my sorrows frozen?
My tears dried up?
There is a large empty space
it is all darkness and silence
yet the waves of destiny roll on and on
their sound is crashing over me.

Where am I to go?
What is there to do?

There are no letters written in the sky
no still, small voice in my heart. Yet from this pain
of separation rush waves of new strength.
What have I done? What is my sin?
Why all these trials?
Was my joy, my exuberance unfounded?
Was it all a dream, illusion, unreal?
Where is hope now? I can't give up hope,
I would rather die.
This body and mind is a burden
I really don't want to carry
if it separates me from the Divine.

Other obstacles creeping in again and again.
I am getting numb
exhausted from the struggle.
Maybe love for the Divine is only an idea.
Am I in love with it?

The power of the experience is so real
it is buried deeply in my mind.
This memory tells me otherwise.
It makes my body shiver just to think
of the sweetness of the flute. What is my love?
Sometimes it is all-absorbing, selfish.
Sometimes it does not ask for anything in return.

IN MY HEART IS A SONG

In my heart is a song
that speaks of my dream
to be forever with You.
It speaks of love unknown
beyond all sense perceptions
a longing too deep to be ever
fulfilled by the fleeting moments
I glimpse of You.

When the world sinks around me
the stars' glimmer brightens
my spirit soars in joy to Your
Heaven, beholding You in delight
and bliss.

The song of my heart
speaks of a thousand hours
in Your presence
vanishing in a few moments.

My song answers Your flute,
Your call to come home
yet I have been a truant
wandering over the world
in search of You.

Now Your maya has lost its
power over me
the pain of your teasing
is ended.
I am at the horizon waiting
for Your chariot to take me home.

WHEN LOVING YOU

When loving you, Divine Mother,
my mind is focused easily on you.
All personality aspects stop
their clatter.
Great endurance is needed
accepting Your challenges
to be victorious.
What has ordinary life to offer?
In marriage?
The mating dance is soon over.
In career, the heart remains empty.
Art in various applications
bypasses the hunger.
The monkeys have eaten the bananas
the mangoes are not ripe yet.
Who is it, that dwells in me
drying up the well of emotions?
Must I go elsewhere
to quench this great thirst?

CREMATION GROUND

My guru didn't send me
to the cremation ground.
He suggested
I think of my own immortality.
In the Himalayan foothills, where the Ganges
is rather narrow
thousands of skulls lay
scattered on the ground
after the snow melts.

The cremation ground
is the place of the heart.
In the ashes of your illusions
you find truth.
Truth is Light.
Light is the highest reality.
That Light makes all things
new and fresh. Fleeting moments.
Nothing is permanent.

WHITE BIRD

Is darkness eternal space and time?
How will I know my place
in the universe?
I don't know who I am
beyond this fragile body.

My mind is like that blackness
where nothing seems to happen.
Dark waters forming a lake,
no moon reflects its silvery light.

This must be the end.
Maybe it is the stillness
before the storm of new creation.

Like the faint glimmer
of a distant star
a thought arises in my mind.
Desire awakens strong and powerful
to create in my mind
a white bird
who will traverse
the space from me to Her.

Beautiful bird, where did you come from?
Where is your home?
Be my divine messenger.

On the wings of the white bird
my spirit soars.

Little bird, perch on Her shoulder,
be near Her heart,
be my receptacle for Her advice and guidance.
Listen, strenuously if necessary.
Don't miss the smallest detail.
Her message means life or death.

My mind has run its gamut
bringing only darkness.

The Mother of this universe will
send some ray of light, whisper
words of comfort and hope.
The mind had its share of power
to no avail
leading me in the dark
valley of sorrow.

Her light will open the door
of my heart.
Is my name not Radha, Cosmic Love?
Am I not Her very own?

UNFINISHED POEM (circa 1965)

I have been confronted with my failings and weaknesses.
My hopes have been dashed, and I have met with betrayal.
It would have been easier to suffer material poverty
than to feel abandoned by you.
All difficulties were willingly carried out
for hearing just once more the flute announcing
maybe, the beginning of transformation.
O divine flute player,
You are no redeemer.
I have created my world, and now must destroy it.
And yet it is Your great love offering me to try again and again,
life after life.

COSMIC INTELLIGENCE

Cosmic Intelligence,
Divine Light,
One Source of Energy-Power.
Many schools of thought
and religion – great diversity.
If all is One, how can this happen?
Who is right? Who has truth?

Nothing is permanent, everything
changes. Who can predict?

Have visions and prophecy a place?

The bird that sings in the morning
is caught by the cat at night.

WHAT IS MASCULINE?

What is masculine?
How to define feminine?
Sometimes God is a father,
human fathers seldom care.

The Goddess manifests
great power, terrible
and loving, Divine Mother
provides what Her children need.

God and father are so remote.
Mother is ever ready
to respond to a longing call, sincerity
She will never forego.

The word of the Divine
is only heard when silence
pervades the mind,
even the mantra will not reign.

Breath is flowing gently
filling the cave of the heart
ready to receive Her divine word.

ENLIGHTENMENT

Enlightenment is experience.
Enlightenment is dying
to the world of conceptualizations,
accumulated ideas,
ignorance and darkness.

Symbolism and metaphor are tools.
The mind wants to cling
to its beliefs.
I don't know, but I believe.

Maya is dazzling
colourful in its display of
emotions gripping, tempting.
Attachment just happens?

LIGHT TRUTH

The original Light
reflections in different pulses.
The countless powers of the Divine.
The Divine Mind's pulsation
after a penetration to the core.
Narrowness, a point of Light.
First the Goddess innate
a sensation of expansion of mind,
then a Goddess of greater dimension.

A path of super-awareness
vigilantly fixed on pure consciousness
regardless of beauty or ugliness,
wrong or right, sensual or mental activities.
Dealing with facts
then desires.
Discrimination, clear Light.
Knowledge of the Divine
appears in its own time, surrender.
Which way to Truth?
Truth is One,
approaches are different.
Awareness is Divine Light shining.
Spiritual and material success — awareness
is the antidote
to failure in both worlds.

TO FIND THE ENTRANCE

To find the entrance
to that hidden place
will demand mental acrobatics
taking risks, destroying concepts
and unproven beliefs
conquering fear of falling from
the rainbow into abyss.

Remember
others before you
have done it, and did walk the rainbow
their search sincere, their longing great
the loving desire gave them strength.

Finally, lifetimes were
not wasted anymore.
The decision made
is crowned by a blessing.
The Pearl of Great Price is won.

DREAM IMAGE

Is consciousness inherent in breath?
Or is it the mind alone that hears?
Has mind experienced it all before?

Mind, my mind, why are you
creating all these tangible and
intangible things?
How do I know what is real
and what phantasmagorical?

Your illusory power
changes its own creation
moment by moment.
So, what is real?

Are these dazzling plays inviting
my emotions, or do they
reinforce the mind's fireworks?

Mind alone creates those
dreams, mind is the
dreamer.

What is the power of my dreams?
Memory from a long forgotten past?
Appearances emerge –
real, unreal,
related or just fragmented?

A beautiful image
that mind conjured.
Where did it come from?
Where will it go?
When will it come back?
Why does it not stay?
Let me hold it so I can be
comfortable, fulfilled.

It cannot be, why not?
How can my heart bear this cruelty
enthralling me for a few brief moments.
Is my mind, my creation
of the Divine, ever new
ever changing, larger and larger,
more and more remote?

Can mind follow its own
creation? But to where?

YOGIS, ADEPTS, EVEN GODS

Yogis, adepts, even gods
adore the Light.
My senses are not willing
to let go of creating an
image of You.
My fancy anticipates
Your Presence
until it dissolves into Light.
Of course You are bodiless
like my essence.
I am not the body, neither a mind.
Am I a spark of Your Light?

THREE WORLDS

Three worlds, all illusion.
Playground of Maya,
mind's selective interpretation.
The bubbles of illusion burst.
Rude awakening.
Pain, tears, even faith
is dying, turned
into intellectual ramifications.
The Light has dimmed too much to find the way back.
So many layers to strip away.

Energy as such
is neither feminine nor masculine.
It is not good or bad, either.
Application changes
decides on the course of evolution.
Creation, destruction
are just changes of Energy-Vibration.

EXCESSIVE HAIRSPLITTING

Excessive hairsplitting
the way of the sporting intellect
to push the right button
evidence of love.

The gift has the wrong wrapper
the ribbon is not the right colour
prison of opinion
so many prisons of self-will.

Ego the builder of prisons
vanity the slanderer of truth
after great thunder
a deep breath, clarity.

I have heard of spiritual concepts
too many to count, what to believe?
To believe is not enough
to know, demands personal experience.

What is my foundation?
Are my building stones
honesty, devotion, humility?
Is sincerity the binding force?

Spiritual experiences come as a loving gift
Divine Mother is ever generous
I must give Her all that I am.
My hands open, receive Her presents.

NO GHOSTS PLEASE

No ghosts please in my subconscious
pride is guarding the door
preventing exit of the thieves
robbing me of liberation.
What am I so afraid of?
Very young, suffering, rejection
was the daily bread.
How can I take more?
A woman surviving in a man's
world has to be charming
catty and deceitful
hiding true feelings of pain.
Don't be a victim of self-deception.
It is better to be with truth in Hell
than with lies in Heaven.

TREES SPLIT, BRANCHES SCATTERED

Tree split, branches
scattered, leaves burned
long ago or was it yesterday?
Damage of earthquakes
cannot be repaired.
Is survival a blessing?
No, no, only when You
tell me softly
You have been with me every
step of the way, never leaving
sight of me, can I let go of fear.

DON'T BE FOOLED BY EMOTIONS

Don't be fooled by emotions.
They are uncultivated,
they are unproven
and yet they are believed.
These illusions are creations
of the untrained mind
assuming speculative philosophy.

In that hidden place on the moon,
the seat of enlightened consciousness,
don't let the clear Light be obscured
by the colours of illusions.

That path is the way to freedom.
That path of superior consciousness
is freedom.

Like the moon has its dark spots
so the mind is clouded
by self-deception and willfulness.

ALL DISSOLVES BACK

Those faculties of thinking, intelligence, understanding
and voicing, expressing, creates a vast difference.
Social, educational standards
had their influence.
Mental capacities of various individuals
mistaken as eternal.
All dissolves back into pure energy.

CONSCIOUSNESS IS WITHOUT SEX

Consciousness is without sex
something is latent, not lost
in the recesses of the mind
smoldering ashes still glow
to light a lamp, to find the way
even a small flame overcomes
darkness.

Light is not enough
action must follow
climbing the path.

THE HIDDEN PLACE

The hidden place on the moon,
the Goddess, the primal Energy,
the Light of Consciousness.
The many names of the Goddess
are only aspects of our approach.
Her powers are comparable to
a musical scale, some
sounds are given their distinctive names.
The masculine Godhead
claims it all.
How can milk flow
from His nipples?

MANY OLD GODS ARE STILL AROUND

Many old gods are still around
wearing different garbs
and masks as times are changing
self-importance grows
authority's impact intensifies.

The rose looks impressive
thorns are big and sharp
tiny ones stick in the skin
the nightingale sings
its last song.

PRIESTS OF ALL SORTS

Priests of all sorts
just command ceremonies
their dogmas — to keep away
those who want to come to You,
to be worshipped like You —
yet they can't fill the heart
with bliss, Your Presence.

Dogma and ritual routine
make Your Presence
only more desirable.

You are already there, here
somewhere
in my heart, my mind
when will the fog clear?
What a paradox
to seek You in form
however beautiful.
My senses don't want
to be starved yet.

Have patience with me.
Every time I look at the mala
of skulls around my neck
I am reminded
of the long journey
of the past.
Should I have arrived
long time ago?

Why do You keep me?
I wish it was only to
serve You a little longer.

RELIGION AS I KNEW IT

Religion as I knew it
stood between me and the Divine.
How could I find my way?

Can one believe what is told?
Words of God – how did they
get into the books?
Faith by intercession
dependency, false security
a dog's leash or golden chain
what's the difference?

I walk naked through the streets
of many countries.
The sun rises in the East.

OH DEVOTEE OF LITTLE INTELLIGENCE

Oh devotee of little intelligence
use your mind, that divine gift.
Discriminate.
What kind of god needs
your protection?
Power-hungry masters
play on your fears and desires.

You can ask your heavenly Father
for bread,
He will not give you stones.
Hear the knock on the door?
You must open from the
inside.

LOVERS HAVE THEIR DREAMS

Lovers have their dreams and expectations.
They hope for eternal spring.
They see happiness everywhere.
They hear music that sounds sweet to the heart.
Their imagination paints pictures,
kindling expectations in ever brighter colours.
This dream belongs to the world of the rainbow,
in the far distance.
Illusory, no solid road leads to it.
The royal highway to life is cemented with reality
that is often painful to walk upon.

MANY HARDSHIPS

Many hardships were encountered
burning in the fire of purification,
it did not leave me without scars.
Words like love, peace, happiness
are missing in my dictionary.

BABIES ARE ATTRACTED

Babies are attracted
by colourful toys.
Divine Mother if
I want to be Your handmaiden
I should let go of the kindness
of reassuring visions.

ARE YOU NOT PAINTING YOUR OWN PICTURE

Are You not painting
Your own picture in my mind?
Who else is it if not
the creative power of Your maya?

DIVINE MOTHER'S MANY FACES

Divine Mother's many faces —
European, Japanese, Chinese, Russian.
Her many names so sweet and melodic,
a crystal appears in different hues reflected in it.

The Earth is one single unit
floating in space, cut up
into many, many pieces
we call countries.
All these different cultures,
human characteristics
fear, anger, humour, pain.

Maya keeping things concealed within
the kernels of the pomegranate.
Pulsation of Consciousness personified
as Goddess, Mother of Earth,
Mother of the Universe,
Light of the Absolute.

The vibrating power of Consciousness
energy to express, create, change.
Destruction.
No split, different variables.
Mental activity during a day — sleep,
thoughts, dreams,
memory — the same power.
Maya, pure energy
in that hidden place of the moon.

The body disintegrates.
The Light of Consciousness will not.

GREAT WISDOM IN DISGUISE

Great wisdom in disguise
of an awesome serpent
crushing illusions, childish plays.
Power of immensity
turning into a dragon
guarding the entrance
of the hidden place.

ENDLESS DESERT

Endless desert, unbearable heat
existence of terror
life without mercy.

Flowers of love and forgiveness
never bloom here
the water of gentleness has dried up.

Sandstorms bury everything
cold wind chills the bones
a streak of silver over the horizon.

WITH GREATER AWARENESS

With greater awareness
comes luminous wisdom
this experience beautiful
and frightening at the same time.

The mind dazzled by supreme ecstasies
refuses to return to a dark
and deceitful world with all
those illusions ending in pain.

Passionate desire for awareness
to be again absorbed in the
splendour of Divine Light
I find the secret place on the moon.

I STOOD BY THE POND

I stood by the pond
looked into its clear water.
Remember little Krishna?
'Please mother let me see
the moon.' Yasoda points
to the reflection in the water.

There is no moon now
but a face beautiful,
gentle, deep, penetrating eyes
like dark suns
shining brightly. Krishna.
What is this? Is it really You
or a projection of my mind?
Your response to my longing
an assurance of Your
everlasting presence?
A white lotus swaying gently.
Memory externalized in
blue lapis swimming a single pearl.
Krishna they call you a thief.
You are a magician too.

DIVINE MOTHER,
WHO HAD THAT GREAT BLESSING

Divine Mother
who had that great blessing
to recognize You first?

Was it in Your terrible form
producing, devouring
by striking thunder?
Or was it in Your beauty
warmth and sweetness?

When I met You first
my heart was a dark
empty cave, my mind
clouded by loneliness
and despair. No mother
but a kind washerwoman
low caste, took me into
her arms, caressing my head.

She, Your manifestation
full of compassion, gave
comfort to the lost child
and later, when agony
took over again
when tradition was given
a share, heart rent
to pieces, all eggs broken.
The voice of authority
roared loud and powerful,

'Your sins, look at your sins.
Be ye perfect as your Father
in Heaven is.'

THE COSMIC DANCE

The cosmic dance
in each life a different costume
variation of steps in a new rhythm.
Speech of many tongues lost
in turning of the cosmic clock.

Have I lived before?
Memory is veiled in fog.
Grace a gift to forget, relief,
pain lessened. Gentle mist
moistens, some images
are soon washed away
lost in time. My identity is murky
to say the least. Who am I to profess
to know? Maybe Light manifests in
many shapes and forms. How many
names did this 'I' answer to?
Each life full of challenges and links
in the chain of evolution.
Thoughts arise powerfully.
I am smaller than a grain of sand or
a star in the universe.

WHERE IS MY HEART?

Where is my heart?
Oh, not the one that beats
when excitement arouses it.
The real heart
that reflects knowledge of
true love without any 'because'
attached to it.

My real heart is
in the hidden place on the moon
where the moon truly reflects
the brilliant Light,
the Divine Source.

Emanations of knowledge,
of great power.
Self-luminous Consciousness.

WHEN YOU FIRST CALLED ME RADHA

When you first called me
'Radha'
my heart leaped literally
my breath stopped
my mind went blank
then a flood of indescribable
joy surged over me.

Being with Krishna can't be
an intellectual event
the fire is mixing in the play of
clever words and mental
acrobatics.
Being with Krishna can only be a passionate
love affair, all consuming
filling every cell of the body
with Krishna's essence.

Radha and Krishna's love, the Cosmic Play
has of course all the ingredients
of a love affair, spiritual
and erotic, aesthetic.

How else can an ordinary human
understand the Cosmic Play?
To be close will always be related
to best closeness experienced by humans.
Lovers think of each other all the time,
in meditation every cell of being is on

the alert, like a lover expecting
the arrival of the beloved.

The separation, the long waiting period.
This power of love is not to be
compared to wifely duties.

SOME SOULS

Some souls are attracted
by glittering luxuries, allowing
indulgences, great passion, selfishness
nourished by pride.
Exaggerated ego demanding
satisfaction at any cost.
Blood flows, heads roll
hearts torn apart. Hunger
and pain are rewards of all
slanderers of compassion.

Returning to the grave gives
no new promise of
paradise. What then?
Where is the purpose of it all,
life after life, if no
purpose is recognized?
Miracle of grace
lightens the blackness that
covered the mind.
Light, some light, any light
would be a blessing for the
killer *and* the survivor.

Light is consciousness,
Divine Light, illumination
a way to Liberation.

Hard-won freedom.
Vibration of heavenly sound,

fire of compassion regenerated.
Light-filled mind and heart.
What better purpose than
to be a bodhisattva?

AFTERWORD

The light comes into my front room in horizontal washes. The season is turning, this year a graciously slow-moving entry into winter. I have spent the autumn working on this collection of Swami Radha's poetry, wandering the city while the leaves change colour and the air gets cooler, with headphones on, listening to her voice. Each step is guided by these poems. They are the atmosphere I breathe. Nine years after Swami Radha's death, I feel closer to her than I have in a very long time.

Swami Radha put this book in motion almost fifteen years ago when she started to collect, edit and record the poems she had been writing since the 1950s. These poems had special significance to her. As a very public spiritual figure and teacher, poetry was a refuge for her, a place to express her pain, her doubt, her love and her longing.

It's a disorienting exercise, however, editing and collecting poems after the author has passed away. There are questions I want to ask that can never be answered; there are stories hidden between the words that I itch to know. I find the clues on scraps of paper or hidden in old files, *this poem was written after… this poem is about a dream… this poem is inspired by a book I read…* but it's all mysterious at best. So my task has been sorting through years of material, trying to get at the heart of what she wanted these to be.

This book also has special significance for me, but I'll get to that later. First, I want to introduce Swami Radha, and give a little background on the influences in her life that inspired these poems.

＊

I knew Swami Radha in her seventies and eighties. At that time in her life, her ashram in Kootenay Bay was flourishing, she had written many books and proven herself, as a woman and a spiritual leader, in times that were not necessarily kind to either. She was fierce, fiery and very intelligent. She read more than anyone I knew, and looked at you with eyes that are indescribable, at once holding you responsible for your truest nature, and loving that nature, with a sincerity I have not encountered since.

I didn't know until my late teens that on top of her writings on yoga philosophy, Swami Radha also wrote poetry. Around that time, I was beginning to get interested in the arts, and began to write poems myself. She would talk quite a lot to me about art, telling me stories about her experience in the art world in Germany before World War II, when poets would pack coffee houses and art, in her opinion, was generally more appreciated than it is today.

She had a successful career in modern dance before the war, and afterwards when she emigrated to Canada. She showed me all her old dance photos, which were movie-star beautiful, and so different from who I knew as Swami Radha. I realized then that this woman, Sylvia Hellman, had led an exotic, fascinating life, beyond what I knew of her as a swami and teacher.

She was born in 1911, the only daughter of a wealthy Berlin family. But those years in Europe were to be full of turmoil, and by the time she was forty, she had seen two world wars, a civil revolution, the loss of her home and most of her possessions, and the deaths of two husbands. The first, Wolfgang, was executed by the Gestapo for helping people to escape Hitler. Her second husband, Albert Hellman, a musician who had composed music for her dancing, suffered a stroke and died at home just eighteen months after they were married.

After Albert's death, Sylvia decided to leave Germany, and in 1951 she landed in Montréal ready to begin again. It was in Montréal that she developed a connection to yoga, and made the first steps on her transformative journey of becoming Radha.

*

As Sylvia Hellman, she had known wealth, love, art, war, pain, tragedy. She came through all of that and wanted one thing – to find the Divine. In 1955 Sylvia traveled to India for the first time, making her way to Rishikesh to meet Swami Sivananda. In him, she found her guru and her inspiration. (The story of their time together is documented in her published journals, *Radha: Diary of a Woman's Search*.)

Less than six months after her arrival, Swami Sivananda initiated her into the sacred order of *sanyas*, and gave her back her old name, Radha. With the initiation she embarked on an entirely new life and purpose. This is also when the poems begin, giving voice to the most personal of relationships, her relationship with the Divine.

The poems trace the story of her spiritual life as Radha, and were written from the late 1950s until the mid '90s, before her death. The significance of the poems, I believe, is in their simplicity and honesty.

Simple, in use of language, so that whole meta-worlds are created in each line. They are at once a sincere expression, and a pointed gem of the purest teachings. Without the addition of artifice, the poems are polished and clear, like diamonds:

> Miracle of grace
> lightens the blackness that
> covered the mind.
> Light, some light, any light
> would be a blessing for the
> killer *and* the survivor.
>
> Light is consciousness,
> Divine Light, illumination
> a way to Liberation.
>
> (*Some Souls*)

And they are honest poems, in the way she offers up her teachings, her love and her most intimate doubts. The amount of questioning is the one aspect of her poetry that surprised me the most. She reveals so much uncertainty, but what it serves to do is catch up the reader in the most human side of a Divine love affair. Who of us has not questioned the purpose of our life, our connection to the Divine?

> Why all these trials?
> Was my joy, my exuberance unfounded?
> Was it all a dream, illusion, unreal?
> Where is hope now? I can't give up hope
> I would rather die.
> This body and mind is a burden

I really don't want to carry
if it separates me from the Divine.
                              (*The Flute*)

Shining through the questioning is what exists
outside of the mind – the devotional heart, cosmic
love – the aspect of the Divine that Radha is named
after. Her heart is in these poems, a questioning heart, a
broken heart, a heart full of Light.

Her light will open the door
of my heart.
Is my name not Radha, Cosmic Love?
Am I not Her very own?
                              (*White Bird*)

Swami Radha's poetic voice is infused with the
intelligence of a life lived with passion. All of her
teachings were informed by her life experiences, before
and after she became Radha. This realism is what makes
them accessible, practical and also inspiring. Her poems
offer another facet into her teachings, and reveal the true
complexity of spiritual experience.

*

I feel the biggest gift Swami Radha left us was the
recordings of these poems. They were recorded in two
sessions over 1991 and 1992. I was living at Yasodhara
Ashram at the time, finishing up grade twelve at the
local high school. My mother had just moved to the
ashram, beginning her own journey of transformation.
(She was to become, in the following years, Swami

Radha's successor, though no one, except maybe Swami Radha, foresaw that change of events.)

I remember seeing my mother just after she sat in on one of the recording sessions. This may sound strange, but she wasn't solid anymore. Her eyes were big and full of Light. She came over to me to give me a hug and a kiss on the cheek, and her flesh had this certain quality to it, softer and lighter than anything I had ever touched, as if my body could pass through her body.

My mother whispered in my ear, *I just listened to Swami Radha read her poems.* And I didn't really know what to say. I just thought, something magical has happened, something must have been transmitted here, something like God or love or the true nature of Radha. I felt in awe and also kind of sad, but a good sad, because I knew that whatever had happened had changed my mother completely, and it was so pretty, the change.

Talking to my mother about it recently, she called the poems "diamond sparks."

"Swami Radha concentrated her whole life, all her spiritual experiences, into these pointed, diamond-sparked poems. Teachings can be transmitted on different levels; it's not all performance and flash. It's the quiet times, too, and you don't even know what it is at the time, until you need it. That's how Swami Radha taught. Often we would just sit at the table with her, talking, being, having silent times."

And it's true. Even though Swami Radha is not here, and the details I desire to know about the poems are not readily revealed, I feel I have spent the last few months sitting with her, walking with her, in conversation, and getting to know her in a very intimate way.

I jumped at the chance to put this collection together. I needed this time with Swami Radha. I think she knew that. Just a couple of months before her death, I gave her a small book of my own poetry, with the inscription: "I give you my writing, which is my life." She replied by sending me a card that said: "To keep this great commitment, you must make every effort to maintain contact with your inner light. But when you need me I will be available, now or in the future."

Through her poetry, she made herself available to me. I know Swami Radha now as a poet, and it is exactly how I needed her – standing in the sun at Parc Mont-Royal, having her words illuminate large parts of my life, then focus down again into sparks of Light.

And while it's a completion of the project, it may also be a beginning, where we can all meet this woman as a poet and hear her voice again. So take these poems, read them, then listen to them, then listen and read along. They will keep unfolding. They are an opportunity to spend some time with Swami Radha. Diamond-spark time.

Clea McDougall
Montréal, October 2004

Typeset in Centaur
Printed and bound at Friesens

Editor
Clea McDougall

Design
Todd Stewart www.breeree.com

Audio
Originally recorded to analogue tape over two sessions
in 1991 and 1992 and digitally re-mastered in 2004 by
Swami Gopalananda at Yasodhara Ashram.

timeless books
Since 1978, **timeless** has been publishing print, audio
and video media that bring alive an ancient lineage of
yogic teachings. **timeless** presents a variety of practical
spiritual tools for daily living. For a free catalogue
contact:

Canada:
P.O. Box 9, Kootenay Bay, BC   V0B 1X0
contact@timeless.org
(800) 661-8711

The United States:
P.O. Box 3543, Spokane, WA   99220-3543
info@timeless.org
(800) 251-9273

www.timeless.org

About the author
Swami Sivananda Radha (1911 – 1995) is the author
of classic books on yoga and spirituality, including
the seminal *Kundalini Yoga for the West* and *Radha: Diary
of a Woman's Search*. She is the founder of Yasodhara
Ashram, and the inspiration for the award-winning
yoga magazine, *ascent*. She is known for her practical and
passionate teachings, which are an intrinsic part of the
yogic tradition in the West.

    Swami Radha devoted her life to yoga, often using
poetic language to articulate her love for the Divine.
The poems collected in this volume are her teachings
at their most personal and precise. They were written
over a period of 40 years, and reveal her most intimate
experiences on the spiritual path.

About the editor
Clea McDougall is a life long disciple of Swami Radha.
She was the editor of *ascent* magazine for over 5 years,
and is now a senior editor at **timeless books**.